First Printing, 2025

EMBERS AND ASHES

Embers and Ashes

JOAN MAYDET

This Book Is Dedicated To:

Momma:

Thank you for always being there for me. I know things were not always easy, and I definitely didn't make them any easier. I understand now, and I'm sorry. I love you so much.

Jane & Richard:

You both have been there since the beginning of my recovery. Thank you for the million ways you have changed my life and supported me through everything. I love you.

Mike:

My best friend. My soulmate. My husband. I've always said since the moment I met you, I knew you were going to be such an important person in my life, I just didn't know how. Thank you for being you. Thank you for being on this journey with me since the beginning. Thank you for loving me and being there for me through some of my darkest times. I'm so glad to be living this amazing, wonderful life with you by my side. Here's to forever! I love you!

Jenna, Anthony, Terri, Paul, Jen, Anglade, & the Amazing Staff at PROS:

Simply put, without out all of you I wouldn't be here. Thank you for helping me find the light. Recovery is hard, but it helps having a wonderful, loving community in your corner.

Contents

Intro

What follows is my mental health recovery journey told in verse covering the years from 2019-2024. Although I have been in recovery for almost six years now, this is just the beginning of my journey, and as you will witness, the journey is far from linear.

It took me years to get help; to stop running from myself and my demons. I almost didn't make it. For anyone who is struggling, please know there is help out there. There is hope. There is a future. There is light through the darkness, even if it doesn't seem like it right at this very moment.

If you, or someone you know is struggling, here are some resources that might be useful to you:

- www.nami.org
- helpline@nami.org
- 1-800-950-NAMI (6264) - Available Monday through Friday, 10AM to 10PM EST
- Text "HelpLine" to 62640 - Available Monday through Friday, 10AM to 10PM EST
- Dial or Text the Suicide Crisis Helpline at 988
- Text HOME to the Crisis Text Line at 741-741

You are not alone,
Joanie

Chapter 1

2019

March 16, 2019

The silence lets the thoughts grow loud

The doubts, these voices

That I still don't know how to live without

The empty air, the quiet house

My thoughts are free to roam

Unannounced

I can't run, I can't hide

There's nothing left to do

Except fight to stay alive

So I drown out the silence

But it's never enough

The silence knows where to find me

These days are so tough

Fight against the silence

Fight against the thoughts

Slowly I am winning

Slowly I won't get lost

March 27, 2019: Mirrors and Smoke

Hide behind a plastic smile

The mask I wear to keep me in denial

The shades I wear to hide my eyes

So you can't see the tears I cried

The quick laugh and the jokes

Are all just mirrors and smoke

A magic act to hide the pain

Are just sunshine hiding rain

If you hold my hand for a little while

Maybe you will see behind the smile

If you glance the real me

I'm afraid of what you might see

Behind the quick laugh and the jokes

Behind the mirrors and the smoke

April 15, 2019

I wear my suit of armor as I ride into the game

It hides the wounds and scars

But words and rumors hit me all the same

The words they hit like knives

As I'm ripped and torn apart

The rumors spread leaving me broken

Shaking in the dark

I wear my suit of armor

But it's never been enough

To reflect the outside world

That to me has always seemed so tough

I'm left feeling bruised and broken

Not able to escape from the pain

But it's my suit of armor

That has saved me all the same

I wear my suit of armor

As I ride into the game

Knowing there are dragons to slay

Hoping I don't get lost

Along the way

And as I march into battle

I know I will be alright

Because beneath my suit of armor

I've always had

An inner light

May 4, 2019

My paper knight
Was bound to break
Even though he tried to remain strong
But minute by minute
And year by year
I committed way to many wrongs.
My paper knight bent and folded
As paper tends to do
I left him crumpled on the floor
As I lay crumpled too.
We both were made of paper
Too fragile for this life
Our strength combined was paper thin
Brutal stab wounds of a knife.
Our paper armour torn in two
Was left in pieces all around
I tried to glue my paper knight

Back together safe and sound.

One day my paper knight

Will start to mend and heal

And eventually he will start to see

His armour is made of steel.

My paper knight will be strong

Just like he was meant to be

And he will forget the paper girl

Who brought him misery.

May 26, 2019

Fate took you by the hand

And led you down a path you never planned

Doors shut tight

Locked with keys

But maybe this was the only way

That I could find me

Forced to grow

Thrown into a world

That was completely cold

Unknown

I saw the shadows as I broke away

Sun was blocked out

For another day

Forced to shout

Forced to fight

Forced to climb

There was such precious little time

To find my way

Lost in the trees

But somehow, someway

I found a way to be free

Scars dot us like patchworked quilts

Meant to keep us safe

But sometimes we need to face the demons

Just to find the reasons

So we open up the doors sealed tight

And see there is no more reason to fight

Just to let go

Just to be free

To find the way back to being me

June 2, 2019

She's heading up a track

She doesn't know where she's going

Insignificant paper girl

Crumpled and torn

Battered and worn

Holding it all together

But the jagged edges are showing

She wants to feel loved

She wants to feel free

But instead she lies on the floor

Saying "these tears might just drown me"

The paper girl is a pile of pages

Written on

Ripped out

Pulled apart

Scattered throughout the ages

She's seen more than she should have

The pain eats her up inside

Yet somehow she continues to survive

To thrive

To hopefully find purpose

As the paper thin pages she's written upon

Begin to take focus

She forgives those who hurt her

But she'll never lose the scars

That only served to make her stronger

That made her want to aim for the stars

But galaxies are distant dreams

That seem just too far away

The paper girl

Looks up and sighs

Tearstained pages of her life

Piercing her dreams like a knife

Bringing her to earth once again

And reminding her

Of where she's always been

Crumpled and torn

Battered and worn

She's heading up a track

She doesn't know where she's going

Insignificant paper girl

Holding it all together

But the jagged edges are showing

June 9, 2019

Don't fall in love with the damaged girl

The one with darkness in her eyes

The one with jagged edges

Who will pierce you with her sighs

Don't fall in love with the damaged girl

The one who can't be saved

You'll try to be her shining knight

But instead find yourself in a cave

One of darkness and no light

You will find yourself screaming

Trying to fight

Don't fall in love with the damaged girl

She is the one you can't save

Just leave her where you found her

And watch her dig her grave

July 3, 2019

You played this game
that I didn't want to see
But slowly, surely
the truth was revealed to me
The truth was written
on the walls all along
But I was blinded
I didn't think I was strong
But darkness lifts
when light breaks through
Revealing truths
unknown to you
And strength finds ways
to show what's inside
Showing you
you don't need to run and hide
Life gets tough

and things go wrong

But now I know

that I am strong

July 17, 2019: Shattered Lives

Love is fragile

Love is strong

Somewhere

Somehow

Something

Went wrong

One small slip

One small slice

Bit by bit

Chops of a knife

Words unsaid

Things kept inside

Little explosions

Broken lives

Memories shattered

Hope, trust, and truth

Pieces of a puzzle

Nothing left to lose

Hearts bleeding

Tears streaming down

But it's time

To look around

Did this mean

A thing to you?

Or was this

Just a game for two?

Did you love me?

Did you care?

Were you ever

Really there?

Questions, answers

Truths and lies

Puzzles left

Of shattered lives

July 24, 2019

Watch me rise from

Where I've fallen

Watch me find the strength

And see that I'm not broken

Watch me find a new way to be

Just watch me

Watch me breathe

Watch me as I spread my wings

Watch me as I try new things

Watch me as I start to explore

I'm going to find myself

I'm going to learn so much more

Just watch me become

Who I'm meant to be

I will find myself

Eventually

No more tears

More smiles, more laughs

I'm going to build memories

I'm going to make them last

I'm going to walk along a new path

I will be stronger

I will have faith

Just watch me as I rise

August 2, 2019: Ships

Two ships that pass in the night
Two souls diverged to different light
Two pieces that used to make up a whole
What happened? Where did time go?
Two bodies that once lay entwined
Two hearts that now are misaligned
Two souls that shared the same dreams
Turns out nothing is quite as it seems.
One body now, one soul, one flight
To find the path she knows is right
To find her hopes, her aims, her dreams
To live out her wildest schemes
One ship that sails in the night
One ship that's heading towards the light.

August 21, 2019: Ebb and Flow

Two months, two days
She is no longer afraid
She's not giving in, she's not giving up
She's trusting and leaving it up to luck
She's found her voice, she's found her wings
Now it's time to do all those things
That bring her fear, that make her quake
It's ok to fall, it's ok to break
Because when she hits the ground
It's in the darkness she will be found
She's going to learn to rise, not fall
She's going to battle and not give in at all
She's going to be a force that's unstoppable
She's going to achieve her dreams, it's possible
When she takes flight she'll know
That she is continuing to grow

She'll learn that life can't be mapped or planned

She just needs to take uncertainty by the hand

She needs to trust and to just let go

And get wrapped up in life's uncertain flow

She needs to trust the voice inside

The one that she's been trying to hide

"Nothing will ever lead you astray

Because you have a voice, you have a say"

She needs to be strong, she will survive

She has so many people on her side

Next it'll be three months, four months, five months, six

She'll be stronger and things will begin to click

Things will start to fall inline

And she'll see she just had to give it time

She will see she just needed to trust and let go

That she needed to trust time to ebb and flow

August 24, 2019

Eyes closed watch me fly

On broken wings these alibis

Fear breaks as I free fall

Life flashes - I see it all

Darkness reins behind my tears

Everything becomes crystal clear

Things make sense like never before

I can't stop it that internal roar

I break free - I am reborn

My heart bleeds beneath these thorns

With new eyes I start to believe

As I give in to life's mystery

September 4, 2019

Trying to color within the lines
Was never for me
I was always meant
To be free
You could never contain me
I was meant to fly
You could never restrain me
I never believed in goodbyes
I'd fight against what I was told
I had to follow my own heart
Even if it broke me
I could always find a new start
I was always strong
I just had to believe
I just lost myself for a few years
Sometimes we need time to grieve
But i've grown strong wings

And gained new sight

And I'm now gazing out

Into a brilliant white light

For once I'm not afraid

For once I'm ready to fly

For once I'm ready to take that leap

And give a new way a try

I won't look back

That's where I've been

I'm going forward

With a grin

I'll take what comes

I've still got my fight

But I know I am strong

And I have an inner light

September 8, 2019

They lived happily ever after

Is how the lies begin

When did the smiles start to hide

The pain you felt within?

When did the laughs and the jokes

Hide the tears behind

Mirrors and smoke?

When did she lose

Who she used to be?

And when did she eventually become me?

The blue or the red pill

Which to take?

And would that be

A bigger mistake?

To have the rose-colored glasses

Ripped from my eyes

To see behind the fairy story

To see all the lies

Am I strong enough

To admit these truths?

Am I wise enough

To chalk it up to my youth?

Can I go back to the beginning

Build a life of my design?

Can I just pull out my pen

And begin "once upon a time..."

Chapter 2

2020

January 23, 2020

For the first time in my life I'm not running

For the first time in my life I'm standing still

I'm letting my feelings flow right through me

For once I'm admitting what is real

I'm not used to being vulnerable

I'm not used to letting the walls come down

I'm not used to this new way of life

I'm not used to this solid ground

I used to hold in all my feelings

Until I felt like I would scream

It was better to wear a mask

And pretend to live the dream

But I don't want to go back to who I was

And how scared and unsure I used to be

I used to think it was easier

Just to bottle up all the memories

But I'm learning different ways of living

Different ways of coping

I find myself laughing and smiling more

And I no longer feel like I am choking

I can breathe, I am free, I am me

And I'm learning that's a good place to be

Still sometimes my mind takes me hostage

But I know that only I hold the key

So I'm starting to deal with the past

And learning to let go

It's going to take time

So I've got to be easy on myself I know

But I'm stronger now

And finally I'm free

From hiding behind the mask

I'm finding it's ok to be me

January 31, 2020: Yellow Brick Road

A black and white life
Trying to stay within the lines
Struggling to live by society's design
A husband, a car, working 9 to 5
White picket fences
Dream ideals didn't make me feel alive
I struggled for air, I struggled to breathe
I yearned to find who I was
And what would make me happy
Living life punching clocks
Trying to blend in
Paying bills, keeping a job
Being one of the flock
But a colorless world was not for me
I needed color, I need more
To be free

Decisions made outside of my hands
I was forced to take a drastic stand
To fight or give up
To live or die
I knew I needed to give it another try
I grabbed for crayons, I grabbed for pens
And I started to color my world again
Slowly at first in blues and grays
Then suddenly there were many different shades
I found a happiness I had not known
And I found that I had grown
A black and white life might be fine for some
But I'm traveling a different path
And I'm having fun
A life of freedom, a life of new things
A life I never ever dreamed
I can't wait to see what the future brings
I know I've come so far
And still have much further to go
But I've landed in Oz

And will follow the yellow brick road.

February 5, 2020: This New Road

Viewing life from different angles

Slowly untying the knots and tangles

Of a life lived but never understood

Of patterns repeated that did me no good

Slowly finding new ways to be

Slowly learning and accepting me

Closing my eyes and taking big leaps

Finding I am no longer one of the sheep

Starting to question and trying to find

Why I stayed so long trapped in my mind?

Why was I so scared to learn to be free?

To admit, let go, and let happiness find me?

Questions asked, maybe always a mystery

Starting to make peace with my history

Steps slowly taken a year ago scared

Never knowing all along I was prepared

To face what was coming along life's path

Finding that there was no plan, no map

Being scared, falling free,

crying, darkness, misery

Finding light, climbing out, laughing, stronger

Finding reasons to be scared no longer

Gaining strength and finding meaning

Finding that changing can be freeing

A year looking back so much has changed

My life in many ways has been rearranged

Miles I have traveled and miles still to go

As I keep on traveling down this new road.

February 9, 2020

Two years ago a decision made

A year ago a path was paved

In dirt, in sand, in the dark

Scared and trembling she embarked

A wild journey towards things unseen

Leading her forward toward new dreams

Breaking free and starting to let go

Discovering sometimes it's not an easy road

Recovery is hard, but she is tougher

She refuses to be a pawn, to suffer

She's found strength and new ways to be

Doors opened up when she found the key

A carousel spinning for far too long

She stepped off to discover she was strong

One year, two - lifetimes it seems

Looking back maybe it was a bad dream.

35 years to suffer, hide, and be scared

Going forward she knows she's prepared

She's faced demons - things that go bump in the night

Nothing can stop her or make her give up the fight

She has blank pages, a future, a story to write

Jumping off the carousel led her towards light

And peace, and understanding

Discovering a new steady landing

She is safe, she is strong

She has pages to fill and the story will be long.

March 1, 2020: Trauma

The trauma wants to make itself be known

It sneaks into the wild recesses of my soul

Wanting me to give it a home

A place to call it's own

But the trauma is not me

The blinders have been pulled off

And now I can see

Behind the troubled shades of grey

There now dawns glorious bright days

Filled with sunshine and laughter

I don't need to be trauma's master

I can learn how to slowly let go and be free

Over time it's amazing how I'm finding me

Trauma pretended to be my friend; to keep me safe

But all it ever did was lock me in a cage

Shut up tight, scared to breathe

Scared to make changes, scared to just be

An internal fire to a darknened room was ignited

And a desire was given room to be brightened

A sword found its way into my hands

I knew I would fight or I'd be damned

To just sit by a moment longer

And give in to someone else's demands

A desire to be free broke the chains

Of trauma's hold that binded me

I fought to find my way

To find myself through another day

An internal struggle I fought to win

I am safe now, this is where my story begins

But trauma still lurks like my enemy

Reminding me of where I could be

Guess what trauma, I have one more card to play...

I have hopes to be completely free of you one day.

March 14, 2020

The paper girl was wrong

She was not paper thin

She just needed to pick up a pen

To see where she began

She noticed the sword

She was handed was sharp

And with careful strokes

She took her mark

On a blank page she started again

"Once upon a time" is how she began

She wrote a new story

One with no fear

One where dragons

And darkness wouldn't dwell here

She decided the truth would be her guide

And no longer would she hide

Behind mirrors and smoke

Behind plastic smiles

And masks that hid the words she spoke

She started to collect the keys

That started to slowly set her free

She found she was forged

of something so strong

Which helped her start to see

A world where she belonged

She was made of Earth and air

Of water and fire

She was made of the elements

She could do anything she dared

She was a daughter

of the sun and moon

Only she was keeping herself cacooned

A paper girl she was no more

She shed that layer

And found who she was at her core.

March 23, 2020

I used to hide behind disguises

Afraid to show the real me

Behind the masks and the smiles

I was afraid of who I could be

I'd lose myself to others

I'd lose myself to fairy tale lies

I'd lose track of the person I longed to be

The real person who I was inside

I'd decorate my branches

And pretend that I was ok

You could never tell looking at me

That inside I was slowly wilting away

I lost all that I valued

I lost all that was real

I bargained with the devil

Never realizing what I lost in the deal

Slowly I came to realize

As the walls came crashing down

That reality was paper thin

It was time for me to grab the crown

I fought for what mattered

I fought for what was real

I learned to slowly let go

Of other people's ideals

I followed what was right for me

And let my heart be my guide

For once I trusted my own voice

The one I had shut off deep inside

I found a life that glimmers

I found people who care

I found a life I hardly knew

Or never dreamed to dare

As I started to bloom

Dreams pierced me like knives

The parts of me what had wilted

Started to come brilliantly to life

Now I stand before you

A tree beginning to bloom

But for the first time I'm not hiding

Or to be the person you assume

I stand before you branches bare

Wholey, humbly, this is me

See the scars beneath the branches

I'm embracing who I can be

I may not be perfect

But I know that is ok

Because trees with scars have stories to tell

They didn't lose their way

My roots grow strong in the ground

I'm solid where I stand

And though storms may batter me

It's in the hard times that I understand

That trees need rain to survive

It's when I begin to grow

Which causes new leaves to take shape

And heal the scars that started to show

I begin to be reborn

I start to heal and mend

And slowly I start to find

I have built myself up again

I am a tree with stories to tell

Scars etched along my bark

But I am strong even without leaves

On this world I will leave my mark.

April 15, 2020

Told in stories

Told through rhymes

The echoes of my journey

The places, the times

The ups and the downs

The moments I cried

Echoes of memories

Forgiving the lies

Every step forward

With strength

I'm consumed

Giving me space

To start making room

To release and let go

With each step I take

I'm heading towards something

Something so great

Trusting my heart

Being my guide

Giving in, releasing

In each moment I reside

Second by second

Never far ahead

I'm learning to be

Not by anxiety be led

A journey, a tale

One to be told

Of a girl who survived

And refused to be sold

April 25, 2020

Warriors are created
They are not born
They are forged by battles
Which make them strong
They are dressed in armor
For wounds are bound to come
But this armor holds more power
Then it does for some
This armor gives them courage
Even if it is not forged of steel
For courage comes from deep inside
And that is even more real
The warriors are given swords
Blessed with strength others will never know
These warriors walk around us
But warriors always lay low
They do not make a fuss

About who they are or where they've been

For warriors are just like you and I

Except they walk along the fringe

They see life a way you never have

And yet they have survived

Because all through those hard years

Even warriors know they need to cry

Warriors are survivors

They wear their scars with pride

Because even warriors know they are better off

By not keeping things bottled up inside

Each day is another battle

A warrior must face

But with sword in hand and wearing armor

They face all challenges with grace.

May 16, 2020: Breadcrumbs

I was small and the world was big and scary.

I started to drop breadcrumbs wherever I went.

So I could always find my way home again.

As a teenager the world became scarier.

I dropped more and more breadcrumbs so I wouldn't get lost.

So I could always find my way.

When I was 20 I was longing to be saved.

I thought I had found an answer.

Slowly I stopped dropping breadcrumbs.

Slowly I lost myself.

Slowly I lost my way.

Until I was in the dark.

Until I was so lost I couldn't find my way out.

I had hit bottom and there was nothing to save me.

As I started making choices and became aware,

As I started chopping down the vines that had grown around me and started blazing a new trail,

I started to find glimpses of light.

And oneday I stumbled across a breadcrumb I had dropped so long ago.

I had forgotten.

I started to follow that trail of breadcrumbs

It led back to me.

I treasure those breadcrumbs and vow to never lose myself again.

Now, as I embark on new chapters of my life, I drop breadcrumbs again

As I blaze these paths yet untaken.

May 24, 2020: Life

Once upon a time is how most stories begin

But hers began with a darkness from within

She never knew life a different way

It had been like that ever since the first day

She was born with a fire and a will to fight

She was born for battles and to bring light

She was handed a sword and a shield to stay safe

She was handed many things but never an escape

She was expected to remain strong and aim true

But years took their toll and the blood started to seep through

She could no longer hide the damage done to her soul

She was tired of fighting and just wanted to reach her goal

A place where she could be safe and free

A place to find just exactly who she could be

The first chapter ended with a tragic fate

She was left shaking trying to skate

In a world that she didn't understand or know

In a new world where no one told her where to go

She struggled and fought and started to lose her way

She wanted everything to stop, to stay

Scared, trembling, yet learning to be free

Shaky steps forward found her eventually

She still had her sword, she still had her power

But she was on shaky ground afraid to bloom, to flower

She slowly started a downward spiral

Which hid the trauma she felt from when she was a child

She thought she was finally in control

But all she was doing was acting out a role

She couldn't see that she was lost in the dark

Or how this path would dull her inner spark

She was young and choices were made

She married, became a wife, she started to let her power fade

She forgot about the sword she had been given

And the inner fight and all the ways she had been driven

She completely forgot who she used to be

She gave it all up, she was so blinded she couldn't see

Fourteen years it took again to find the light

And to see how far she had fallen into the night

Fourteen years of pieces to put back together

To find herself and see what she could weather

As she picked up the pieces she started to find

Remnants of a person, a life she had forgotten in her mind

Early on she came across the sword and a key

Which unlocked forgotten doors that hid who she could be

She flung them open and she let in light

She started to find the will to fight

She found new places new ways to be

She found new paths to follow new places to see

She challenged herself like she never had before

She finally started to open all those doors

A year later she is surrounded in love

A year later she has risen above

A year later she has come so far

In just one year she has set a new bar

She stands now with her sword held high

With her face turned towards the sun in the sky

May 28, 2020: Dreams

He wrote his dreams on a Post-It note

Not able to see what he had before him

Not able to see that one of his dreams

Was real

And not a dream after all.

She read that list over and over again

And it tore at her heart

Young as she was

And she vowed to never be like him

To never let her dreams only exist

On a tiny fragment of paper.

September 25, 2020

I've danced along the edges

Brilliantly bursting into flames

I've descended into ashes

This life became a game

Of survival

Hide

Behind

Smiles

Suffer in silence

Don't let anyone see

How you bleed

How you ache

Don't admit what you need...

Still

Eventually

You break

There's only so much

You can take

And I'm grateful for that fall

For the clarity

To see beyond it all

For the strength it took

To finally come alive

For the strength it took

To thrive

For the uphill journey

And the doors I blew open

For taking candles

To shine light

Behind dark curtains

For the journey

That led me here

Mountains of memories

And this life of no fear

Where I am so safe

And cared for

For feelings I've never

Felt before

For love that is deep

And true and strong

Knowing I'm supported

Life can be beautiful

Life can be like a song

Seeing the light

Instead of the dark

No longer dancing

Along edges

On this new path

I choose to embark

No longer hiding

Behind smiles

No longer playing

Those old games

Today I dance in the light

I dance in the flames

Thankful

Grateful

Blessed

October 7, 2020

The mirror streaked

Reflecting broken dreams

Cracked and smashed

It had no sheen

Tarnished

Dusty

A treasure decayed

I deserved more

Than to live this way

I picked myself up

From the floor

Where I'd fallen

I brushed myself off

No more of my life would be stolen

I stepped through the glass

Of dark and despair

To find a life

That matters
And where people care
To be present now
I need to glance back
It helps to remind me
I'm on the right track
To be mindful
Grateful
Proud and sure
I remind myself
Of the battles I fought
The reason I fought this war
I was important
It was me who mattered most
Because in that other world
I had become a living ghost
I live everyday now
So grateful to be alive
I fought so hard to be here
To have people who love me

By my side

I fought for my dreams

I fought for me

And so I am grateful

For each minute

I just get to be.

November 6, 2020: Bloom

The other side unknown

Among chaos was how she'd grown

A weed just trying to bloom

In a dark place with no room

Struggling just to find light

Not trying to give into the fright

Only living what she knew

And in this place is where she grew

She broke free as soon as she could

But you can't outrun your childhood

You can only run so far so fast

But eventually you catch up to your past

Knowing things needed to change

Finding life had to rearrange

Growing through the doubt and pain

Letting tears fall like silent rain

No longer running, standing still

Doing the hard work, heading uphill

Working on staying here and now

Never giving up no matter what or how

Never again to be locked in a dark room

Never again to be a weed just trying to bloom

December 11, 2020: Wild Unknown

Stepping out

into the wild unknown

I'm free I'm flying

So much is being shown

I'm like a newborn child

Discovering everything new

My eyes have been opened

Life has taken on a new hue

Life is a wild

Unknown mystery

I just keep going

step by step

Writing my own history

Knowing my path

Is blazing with possibilities

No map, no compass, no guide

On me myself

I've learned to rely

And it's a wonder

In this wild unknown

All the amazing ways

To find that I have grown

So I keep on going

Gathering new skills

I keep exploring

Loving how living feels

And I practice just learning

How to let go and be

How to close my eyes

And learn how to actually see

This wild unknown

Is the journey I've searched for

My entire life

It's one I stumbled upon

Accidentally

When my world was split apart

By the jagged edges of a knife

But I picked up the pieces

And started anew

So proud of myself

For creating a life

And a version of me

That I could be proud of too.

December 30, 2020: Rule of Three

You struck a match

You lit a flame

The gaslights burned

You laid the blame

You twisted words

You made up lies

Swearing truth

You wrote your alibis

You pointed fingers

The witch will burn

Your lies will haunt you

Karma gets its turn

What you put out

Comes back in threes

Be careful where

You send your energy

Chapter 3

2021

January 13, 2021

I used to be the girl

Who unwittingly

Flicked the match

And watched herself burn

Embers enchantingly dancing

In the night

I used to be the girl

Who would arise

From the ashes

Over and over again

Saying she was stronger and wiser

But only repeating

The same mistakes

I used to be the girl

Who died a thousand deaths

Now I am the girl
Who flies; who soars
Who walks away from the fire
And the lure of the flames

Now I am the girl
Who is in charge of her own story
The girl who chooses
To live and be in each moment
Proud of every small step taken

Now I am the girl
Who lives a thousand lives

January 29, 2021

Silence and shadows
Haunting my dreams
Silence and shadows
Hauntingly serene
Lullabies singing
Me softly to sleep
Lullabies singing
Reaching too deep
Like silence and shadows
Will often do
Weaving their deadly spells
Bending what's true
Lullabies singing
I start to agree
Falling through tunnels
Becoming lost at sea
Silence and shadows

Can I find my own way?

With shadows to lead me

Surviving another day

The silence calls me

It is so loud

The lullabies sing

Lost in a cloud

Shadows and silence

I start to give in

Shadows and silence

Should I let them win?

Lost and confused

A voice rings true

Calling my name

A light comes shining through

You're holding my candle

You hold out your hand

I look at you standing there

I begin to understand

I'm not alone on this journey

You are by my side

You'll be my anchor

Together we'll take this ride

Silence and shadows

They can weave their lies

I will help defeat yours

Together we wont listen to

Their lullabies

March 31, 2021: Roots

Dream awake

Dream asleep

The pivotal moment

I decided to speak

A spark ignited

That couldn't be tamed

I knew then

There was no other way

My dreams were too big

But been silenced too long

I had been squashed

I had lost my song

The spark was dying

Slowly was an ember

Time was not on my side

An inner part of me knew

I needed to remember

So it spoke

And it drove me

With an intense drive

Knowing I was meant for more

Than to just "survive"

Who knew the seeds planted then

Would grow such thick roots?

Who knew back then

What those dreams would produce?

Dream awake

Dream asleep

Always grateful

For the pivotal moment

I decided to speak

April 11, 2021: Rabbit Holes

I'm getting lost down rabbit holes

In the silence

In the darkness

My mind takes trips to places

I much rather not go

The darkness summons demons

Who dwell within the deep

They thrive on the silence

When it's sleep that I seek

So I stumble and fall

Down these dark narrow holes

Twisting and tumbling

As I fall far below

My brain weaving scenes

Anxiety takes the wheel

And so I hold on very tight

For all the emotions that I feel

April 18, 2021: Life's Gift

Always on the ready
Always on the go
When you're on a sinking ship
Time does not have a linear flow

Always with a battle plan
Ever vigilant to all around
The girl's mind couldn't take a break
It could never just slow down

The present wasn't relevant
The future was to be feared
The past needed to be remembered
No time to disappear

To her thoughts or to her dreams

She just needed to survive

The present gift unheard of

It was just a bunch of lies

But you can't run forever

Eventually you will fall

Living 0 to 100

Eventually she hit a wall

She fell into the darkness

She could no longer see

Something needed to change

She needed to be free

From the darkness she would rise

Anew she gained sight

She learned how precious every moment was

And learned to bathe within the light

She treasured the gift of living

She treasured the gift of each day

When you nearly lose everything

You don’t want any moment to slip away

May 18, 2021: Ex-Phoenix

Thirty-four I felt dead inside
Was this all there was to life?
Did I reach the end of the ride?
I remember feeling like I was done
Like my time had run out
I'd never get to be "someone"
I had no clue
Who I was anymore
I was just surrounded
By so many locked doors
I cried to be heard
I'd scream, I'd yell
Yet nobody saved me
As into the darkness I fell
The pain was deep
It cut like a knife

But it had become a friend

One I had known for life

I was tired, unsure

But I wanted to live

To break the chains

To love myself and forgive

So I made a bold move

And I took a huge leap

Although it was scary

No longer would I live half asleep

Fast forward two years

I'm thirty-six and still alive

I have come so far

It surprises me how I thrive

My life has changed

From night to day

It's just so amazing

How I see life in different ways

The journey is long

Forever twists and turns

But the fight is worth every step

No longer do I burn

June 9, 2021: Flicker

I don't ever want to be

Someone's little disaster

And I guess that's how I used to feel

Careening off the tracks

Faster and faster

Now I just want to live free

Glowing in my light

I want to be the best version of me

Never giving up the good fight

Still I have my jagged edges

I'm a constant work of art

I am who I am meant to be

A rebellious flicker against the dark

June 21, 2021: Surf

When I'm lost

When I'm found

When silence

Is the loudest sound

When thoughts

Fill my head

When my heart pounds

Filling me with dread

When the tears fall

Like acid rain

When darkness hits

Drowning me with pain

I won't run

From the crashing tide

I will surf this wave

Survive - stand up

Make it to the other side

I will sail to the shore

Determined and free

Knowing nothing

Not even my own mind

Can ever beat me

July 7, 2021:
Beyond

I've cleared away the jagged edges

I've made it smooth and clear

I tried to invite you beyond the mirror

I've tried to show you my inner fears

I've tried to take you beyond the reflection

Beyond what you believe you see

I've tried to take you into the deepest depths

So you could truly understand me

But you want the reflection

The perfectly packaged pose

You don't want to see beyond the mask

Into what the darkness truly holds

You don't want to see the demons

That I fight every single day

You rather believe the smiles

And the shadows the mask hides away

You rather see the surface

Glittering, smiling, nothing out of place

You refuse to look below the surface

Into the hidden darker space

You refuse to take the journey

Deep within my hidden depths

Where the daily work is done

Where demons are slayed; laid to rest

A place of no sleep

For the weary or the wise

It's the place where you get up each day

And constantly give recovery a try

A life of commitment

Two steps forward, one step back

Repeat again and again and again

Always aiming to stay on the right track

The mask hides the work

I commit to every single day

But that doesn't mean life is easy

Or that I need to put up with what you say

Recovery is also learning

To do what is right for me

Sometimes that is taking a step back

Sometimes that is taking a moment to breathe

And sometimes it's just knowing

That I have the right to say "no"

This is my life now

And I can say where I want to go

So maybe you don't understand

And maybe you never really will

The mask brings you comfort

And you believe everything is solved with a pill

At the end of the day I know the truth

While you point your finger saying I refuse to change

Yet I'm the one who invited you beyond the mirror

It's up to you if you want your image to be rearranged

July 27, 2021: Through the Darkness

The pencil does not write

The pen has no ink

A drought has come to the inkwell

The monsters do not speak

The paper is crumbled and parched

White bleached pages left in the sun

She has learned to stand still

The writer finds she no longer has to run

She has found where she is happy

One in which she is safe

She doesn't need to write herself away

To fill up all that empty space

She can breathe now that she's free

Tears now replaced by laughter

Sea-drenched air kisses her face

Turns out monsters can find happily ever afters

August 13, 2021: The Journey So Far

She sold the illusion

She hid behind the dream

Of picket fence nightmares

Nothing was quite what it seemed

She bought into the notions

She bought into the lies

It's easy just to smile

Inside she slowly dies

She learned to be quiet

She learned who to be

Don't create too many waves

Don't let anybody see

Beyond the pretty curtain

Beyond the pretty lies

Picture perfect memories

Now seen through new eyes

Darkness fills the canvas

Silence haunts the scene

Crying out and screaming

Waiting for someone to intervene

She didn't see the exit

All the signs; yet she stayed

When abuse is all you've known

What other choice could she have made?

But fate saw she needed more

And helped her find her voice

When all was darkness and so unknown

Light showed her a choice

A beacon flickering in the dark

So scary and unknown

Yet she grabbed that flickering candle

Knowing it was a sign she had been shown

And thus began her journey

Out of the darkness into light

That step-by-step hard climb

Of recovery, forgiveness, love, and never giving up the fight

August 24, 2021: When Panic Attacks

The treacherous brain

How easily it handed over the controls

My body invaded

No longer acting of its free will

I'm a live wire

Zaps electrify my body

Thoughts spinning

I'm scared

Paralyzed

August 30, 2021: Stronger

Each day I'm getting stronger
A butterfly emerging from a cocoon
I'm surprising myself by new steps taken
Embracing all my phases like the moon
Shining brightly even in dark spaces
I navigate my way through
Though it can be scary and I'm weary
It's time to make my grand debut
It's the small steps taken
That add up over time
It's the tears and the pain
But it's never losing the will to climb
Sometimes it's one step forward
And two more back
But it's always knowing
That I'm on the right track

It's the fight that keeps me going

Making me want to persevere

I've come so far already

Even though so much is still unclear

I try to stay within the present

Live my life just for today

Anxiety and depression have stolen so much

I refuse to give my future to shades of gray

So I own my power

As I emerge from my cocoon

Stronger with each passing day

Stronger with every moon

September 17, 2021: Embers and Ashes

She was embers and ashes

Thoughts burning on a page

She was an unfinished chapter

A character never featured center-stage

She was starts and endings

All she knew was to run

She was a Phoenix rising

Too hot for the sun

She was stuck in a circle

Repeating mistakes over again

She was on a rollercoaster

One with no beginning or end

She rode in circles

She couldn't find a way out

All she had to hold on to

Was self hatred and doubt

She burned and she hated

Who she had become

But she thought for her

Her story was finished - done

But strange things happen

As they often do

Unprepared thrown into the darkness

Her hidden light came shining through

The rollercoaster had stopped

The flames did too

In her hands she held a sword

Its strength making her feel brand new

She was in charge now

The author now held the pen

She could begin a new chapter

Deciding each beginning, middle, and end

She had choices she had freedom

She had hope and so much more

And never will she return

To the embers and ashes she was before

September 27, 2021

Six letters that defined my life

Six letters that caused me strife

Six letters I shed like a snake

Six letters I left in my wake

A new person I would become

My past would fade like a distant sun

But a house of cards is what I built

A house that slowly began to tilt

I lost myself and lost my way

To the shiny new person I tried to play

The six letters that tied me to you

I didn't know I was running from myself too

When the house shattered and slowly fell

I found myself in the darkest well

Six letters found their way back to me

But now they showed me who I could be

The six letters were not a curse

A realization born of time and the universe

With new eyes I now could see

I no longer had to run - I could just be

The six letters spoke of strength

They spoke of survival at any length

They spoke of power that overcame fear

They spoke of ways to persevere

They spoke of those who came before

Of being "beloved" and so much more

Reclaiming who I was meant to be

Reclaiming you and reclaiming me

November 1, 2021

Once upon a time

Was a nice way to start

But it's all lies that eventually

Tumble apart

I live in reality now

No longer in the lies

I prefer to see the truth

Rather than through shielded eyes

I lived in the dark

Wearing smiles

Hiding in laughter

But I found the truth

There was no

Happily ever after

I had to break through the spell

The lies that I was fed

I had to battle with the wicked

To find a path which I could tread

I found that I could be

The hero of my own story

It was I who held the pen

I could shine in my own glory

So I battled with the dragons

With my demons and my fears

And I came out even stronger

Wiser with each passing year

I awoke with a new light

A strongness in my heart

Knowing that not even the darkness

Could ever rip me apart

I've learned the best stories

Sometimes begin with the greatest disaster

Now I know I don't need a fake fairy tale

To live my happily ever after

December 24, 2021

You broke me slowly

Filling me with lies

You made me doubt myself

Who I was inside

And I slowly felt myself fade away

Losing all my color

Giving in to shades of gray

I slowly found myself a dust-lined page

Only a sideline in your masquerade

And as I broke in jagged little pieces

I watched you walk away

Protected by the lies of your charade

Your perfect little escapade

Chapter 4

2022

January 10, 2022: Journey

A flicker in the dark

While I was drowning at sea

That small burst of inspiration

Was the only thing that saved me

A decision made

With hardly a plan

Trusting the Universe

Would hold out it's hand

Scary and dark

The journey turned out to be

But it's the journey that led

Back here to me

Twist turns and falls

Memories ricochet

But I keep learning much more

With each passing day

I never want to go back

To the girl I used to be

Because now I've finally learned

How to be truly free

The path isn't linear

And I wouldn't want it to be

You need to have the dips and falls

To appreciate the highs and ecstasy

That life has to offer

So take the good and the bad

It's a rollercoaster journey

But the best life I've ever had

February 20, 2022

It scares her to think of the girl she was before.

Before her world collapsed.

Before she dared to allow herself to want more.

It scares her to remember all the pain and all those tears.

All the loneliness behind the smiles.

What she hid from everyone throughout those years.

It scares her to think what could have been if nothing changed.

If life didn't happen like it did.

If it didn't force her to take control of the reigns.

And she is so grateful for the path that led her here.

Even though it got dark and scary.

She is grateful for those years.

Now she looks around and is amazed at everything she's gained.

There's only sunlight now, no darkness.

Rainbows instead of rain.

April 18, 2022: Unshaken

I got lost in the shadows

In the dark I lost my way

I got so completely lost

I lost track of the days

I slowly lost sight

Of the person I used to be

When I gave up my name

I gave up a big part of me

I fell and I fell

Into the darkness below

Until I hit rock bottom

And had nowhere else to go

By then it was too late

I was trapped, I couldn't be free

Little did I know more loss

Would help me find the key

I didn't know my tears
Were unlocking hidden doors
I didn't know what
The future had in store
I just had to trust
The hope that bloomed inside
And trust that inner light
That became my inner guide
I shed the loss and processed
The person I had become
I realized I was stronger
My world was full of light and shining sun
And as I stood in this new light
I thought back through the path taken
The darkness the tears the loss the climb
Through it all I remained unshaken

June 6, 2022: Legacy

Connected

By blood by familial ties

By mental illness

By things we can't hide

But no longer do I run

No longer do I deny

I can do things differently

Than you

I can live - I can try

I can get help

Let love be my guide

I can have a community

I can trust - have people by my side

I can grow and change

Heal in ways you never could

I can be the person I want to be

Live the life that I always should

I can thrive in the sun

Instead of shrivel in the dark

I can live each day to it's fullest

Knowing somehow I made my mark

And above all I can know I made peace

Between you and between me

Because although we are same and different

I stepped from your shadow

And finally chose to be free

June 20, 2022

Invisible scars mar my body
Traumas tattooed on my soul
Living in moments free-flowing
Thoughts come and they go
Time like a beacon
Marking chapters of my life
Close the book and look forward
The future is so bright
Heal the scars, see the beauty
Wear the tattoos with pride
Trauma is your companion
Knowledge and wisdom are your guide
Blank pages to fill with memories
A life to heal and be
Discover the beauty of believing
Discover the beauty to be me

July 16, 2022: The Sculptor

You were a careful artist

Chipping away day by day

And I was your willing naïve

Moldable little prey

You worked with care

You worked with ease

I never caught on

You became a disease

You molded and shaped

Who you wanted me to be

Left me confused and shaken

Doubting not knowing I could be free

This was my life

Bound, cuffed but I didn't see the chains

While you carefully hid your smile

And held the reigns

And you watched me suffer

And you watched me die

Gaining pleasure from my demise

And when there was nothing left of me

You threw your cruel tools aside

You were done

You had had your fun

You packed your kit

And left me there

In many states of disrepair

But you didn't count on the strength

The power of me

You didn't know I'd carve myself free

With tools and courage on my own

I found myself

As I carved through stone

I reclaimed the person I was inside

I gained the skills I needed

To survive

And now I am a walking piece of art

A statue come alive

Made up of many parts

I am healing and growing

I've crushed you in my wake

All those lost years

Lessons learned through mistake

Your path I will never cross again

And thankfully you were not my end

August 29, 2022: Brain Games

Hard-wired in my brain

Encoded in my veins

This melancholy game

I am both one and the same

Quick smiles and the laughs

Tears pour down from the past

Memories trump out all the light

Visions coming alive only at night

A rollercoaster ride

Loved ones by my side

I am not on this journey alone

I am safe, I have a home

Breaking through memories and fears

I am present, I am here

Putting a voice to what I feel

Remembering not all my thoughts are real

This is a wild and scary game

Living with this brain

September 11, 2022: 1999

I want to hold you fourteen

I want to tell you everything will be alright

I want to brush away your tears

And tell you not to fear the night

I want to stop the torment

That I know you feel inside

Own your story fourteen

There is no more need to hide

Let go

And just be

The games played

Are history

Let go

And be free

Fourteen it's time

To stand up and find me

Twenty-three years have passed since then

I still see it all so clear

The memories and the feelings

I know how that fourteen year old girl feels

But I'm thirty-seven now

How I've grown and how I've changed

But that fourteen year old girl

Still cries when she hears your name

Let go

And just be

The games played

Are history

Let go

And be free

My unsolved mystery

October 31, 2022

If I could go back
What would I say
To the little girl
Who lost her way
Twenty years running
From fears and could be's
Not knowing she held the keys
That would unlock all the chains
And let her be free
To open oneself up
To the pain, loss, and fear
And finally stand in one place
For the first time in years
It's scary to open up
Let down the gates, open the door
But once she did she found a life
That was worth fighting for

She felt all the darkness

She felt all the light

She felt possibility

There was nothing to fight

Surrounded by love

Safe for the first time in so long

She surrendered with a sigh

Her soul beat with a new song

She felt light and lifted

Just like she could fly

Given new wings and skills

She took to the skies

Little lost girl

So long running away

Twenty years lost

Finally learning to stay

December 5, 2022

Lost amongst the darkness

Thoughts that are not your own

Shifting through the reality

That has become your home

Make it through another day

Paint the canvas bright

No one can see beyond the facade

The story you were careful to write

But what happens when it all crumbles

Faced with the starkness of what's true?

What happens when cold hard reality

Is all that's left for you?

Let your walls come down now

Let your anger go

Open your heart towards healing

It's a long road; take it slow

Chapter 5

2023

February 5, 2023: Looking Back

Show my story

Take you there

Imagine four years ago

A monochrome wasteland

Of despair

It's where I started

But not where I stayed

I was a weed that flowered

Not meant for the shade

I grew from my tears

Of power and change

I grew from persistence

I grew from the pain

Colors started to filter

Into my life

Things slowly looked less bleak

Slowly there started to emerge light

I live along the fringes

And with that I'm ok

The 9-5 daily grind

Never worked for me anyway

I flower and I thrive today

I live a life I love

I'm thankful for the path I walk

And for the ways I rose above

Color fills my life

Hope fills my days

I am fully alive

And that feels good to say

February 27, 2023: Shades

Black was my life before

A dark cave full of despair and longing

Pulling me deeper into its endless depths

Into a world of nothingness

Grey was my world when I started to find hope

Light gently drifting through darkness

Starting to offer me a path

A way forward

White was the blinding light of strength

Showing me that I survived

That the dark was not going to win

It started to color my days

And now I am bathed in colors everyday

Walking and thriving in life no longer afraid

Recovering and fighting my demons

So I can be free

May 1, 2023: Seas of Change

Short Story

A What do you do when you become lost? The darkness was so thick it surrounded the girl. In fact, she couldn't remember the last time she had seen light. She had forgotten what it looked like, what it felt like, the way it could warm you up inside, make you feel alive. The girl was slowly dying by darkness, alone in a sea with no hope of rescue.

When was the last time she ate? When was the last time she spoke to someone? She was too tired to think. She closed her eyes, lying in a fetal position, pulling the blankets up around her, and tried to fall back into the endless darkness.

Maybe she had always been lost. She couldn't remember the last time her feet had touched solid ground. When had she last smiled and laughed genuinely? She usually wore her "Good-Ship-Lollipop" mask acting like everything was ok - perfect even. But, she couldn't do that anymore. She had no energy. Her boat had finally slammed into the rocky shore and was sinking fast, with her aboard.

She needed to do something. She wanted to live. She needed this black mass to ebb and give her some breathing room. She needed to think, to rally herself for what she was about to do. She had a chance, and maybe finally she had an answer.

The girl had been waging a war with this endless darkness for as long as she could remember. She got truly lost as a teenager and just never found her way out. Thirty-four long years of darkness, of fighting against rough seas. It had taken it's toll.

This program offered hope. She had to give it a try, no matter how battle-worn and tired that she was. Her mind shrouded in darkness, she took her first steps forward. To try something new is scary. To change is scary. But the darkness had taken too much from her. It was time to fight.

She attended classes. She attended therapies. She let the lessons and words drift over her and seep into her brain. The girl was afraid to interact with others in the program. She kept her distance. She wore her mask. But everyday she showed up with her sword in hand ready to go toe to toe with the darkness.

Slowly... very slowly she found the darkness was not quite as heavy. She found herself opening up. She found herself talking to others, letting down her mask. It was like a life preserver had been tossed to her finally. She was no longer alone.

She started to take command of her little boat, steering it away from the rocky shores towards calmer waters. She clung to that life preserver, and with shaky first steps she started on her path towards recovery.

May 14, 2023: Skeletons

The place where secrets used to be kept
Under lock and key
The place where darkness and nightmares met
A place not unknown to me
A place I dared not to enter
For fear of what I'd find
A place always front and center
But hidden from my mind
And in this space skeletons hung
Collecting dust; rotting away
And so I struggled walking among
Not knowing my mind was filling with decay
Until I happened upon the door
Forgotten about, opened with surprise
To find cold truths laid out on the floor
Skeletons I began to see with new eyes

I summoned a light and dug into the mess

To see what I could find

Uncovering all that I repressed

I found a path back to my own mind

And through hard work and lots of tears

The skeletons have been tossed

I have freed myself from the darkness years

And from everything I had lost

July 31, 2023

The pen is mightier than the sword
Or at least that's how the saying goes
But maybe it's the sword
That's mightier than the pen
Who leaves all of its thoughts exposed
Upon blank pages for all to read
And think of what they will
But the sword stays quiet gleaming
Conveying strength, but keeping still
The pen moves wildly all about
Leaving ink blots in its wake
But the sword stays there humbly silent
Knowing his presence can make others quake
The sword is mightier than the pen
Mysterious, bold, and true
Never letting his thoughts be known
Except maybe to a chosen few

August 13, 2023: Evolution

I used to be lost

Writing my story

Upon crumbled destroyed paper

Using pencil I erased my thoughts

In anger

Leaving smudged marks

Of what once was

Burning bridges

But never quite escaping

Today I write my story with pen

Inking a new life

Rewriting the narrative

On smooth heavy paper

Filled with promises

Living life on my terms

Building bridges

No longer trying to run

I stand still

Breathing in this life

I love

Pencil vs pen

I rather ink my life

Permanently

September 25, 2023: Midnight

Wild thoughts blow open doors

In dark places which hold power

Repeated lies left to die

Which will wilt and never flower

Breezes shift light lifts

Keeping monsters at bay

Down a pill keep your will

So you can sleep another day

October 2, 2023: The Crow

Lessons learned through time and space

The demon now been given a face

No longer smoke

Silently rattling a cage

No longer falling so easily

To its powerful rage

No longer caught

In a losing game

No longer lost

No longer the same

The demon has evolved

The cage now unlocked

The demon is loved

The demon found grace

Emerging anew

Learning to grow

No longer a demon

Emerging a crow

With strong wings to fly

An inquisitive mind

Adaptive and seen

She takes to the sky

Strong and able

She has been reborn

As she bathes in the light

Of each coming dawn

November 13, 2023

Every day ebbs and every day flows

Riding tides as they come and go

Building a ship that's strong and true

Survive every battle; sail through the blue

Strong sails to face every incoming storm

Strong sails that can instantly transform

Into whatever you need as the situation calls

For life is full of unknowns and free-falls

But a strong ship can sail into any situation

A strong ship just needs a solid foundation

November 20, 2023

I took off my running shoes

And embraced life

Instead of wishing for death

I sought out the light

Learning ways to live

Through every breath

And your ghost

Stopped haunting me

And through the following years

I leaned into recovery

Grateful for every step

I look at my life now

So night and day

From when I was lost in the depths

I know you

Are watching over me

I try to live in the moments

I try to live in the days

Embracing all the love that surrounds me

The light that constantly shows me the way

November 30, 2023

Are you sure you want to venture

Into the dark recesses of my mind?

It's not for the faint hearted

It's made that way by design

It's a place full of mazes

One can easily get lost

It's a place full of demons

Things that must never be crossed

It's where it rains constantly

With tears that never end

Showing movies of memories

That play on and on over again

And it's where I built my walls

To keep myself safe

It's where I lived for far too long

It's where I could never escape

No light reaches

This place full of fears

No light can pierce this darkness

That was built over many years

It's why this place stays locked

Behind vaults, keys, and chains

No one can survive there

It leaves no remains

It's the place of voices screaming

Loud but you're alone

A place that you will never feel

Loved, at peace, or at home

And it's why I learned to seal this place

And build a place of light

It's why I refuse to live

Within that place of night

But sometimes demons

Work their way through

Sometimes dark and light battle

As fearsome forces do

But the dark will never win

I now have too much light

Too much to live for now

To give into this fight

And so I step forward with my sword

Showing the darkness where it belongs

And I stand proud in the shining light

Knowing that I am brave and very strong

Chapter 6

2024

January 6, 2024

Peeling layers off my skin

I'm an onion revealing tears

The deeper you cut away within

Trauma, stories, things never spoken

There are stories here

Slowly being woken

Memories too raw to peel

Things I'm not ready

Yet to touch or feel

Healing slowly in my grace

Peeling onions

Tears silently leave their trace

January 27, 2024: Dreams

Nobody said it would be easy

But that's the path I chose

I never was meant to be ordinary

I was full of dreams left unexposed

I was meant to chase my demons

See myself in unexpected ways

I was meant to smash the mirror

And to see beyond my days

Everyday is still a puzzle

Pieces I'm trying to fit in place

Take responsibility for my actions

Know this journey is not a race

Know that I am still a dream in progress

Proud of how far I have come

Yet I've got miles still to go now

My learning and growing is never done

I know that the wheels still are spinning
Even when I lose my grace
When I hurt or say the wrong things
All the times I fall flat on my face
Yet this is all part of the growing
Part of the path I chose to walk
Pretty words on a piece of paper
But I need to put action behind the talk
So I take small steps each day
Reframe, breathe, and redefine
And as this new world starts to take shape
All my dreams will start to become mine

March 24, 2024:
Free

It's the tick-tock of the clock

The moving passage of time

The juxtaposition of light and dark

Fitting together and finding the rhyme

Its the getting lost

Not being able to breathe

And still screaming out loud

It's the questions and silences

And voids and answers

Of which you start to allow

It's the laughing and crying

And singing and painting

Finding yourself within

It's the moments

Where you catch yourself

Just smiling and seeing everything begin

And you find yourself

Somewhere, somehow

Where you've always wanted to be

It's in these fragile little moments

Between light and dark; breath and silence

Where one truly becomes free

April 1, 2024

We are blank canvases

That ebb and flow with time

Gently being filled with color

Sometimes going outside the lines

We are riots of splashes

Both of lights and darks

We are incredible beautiful

Hard to grasp sparks

We are delicate fragile

Pieces of art

We are unique and we are beautiful

Each and of its own

We are all on journeys

Each trying to find their home

Time wounds and time heals

But we find ourselves again

We come back to our blank canvases

And write our stories in pen

April 25, 2024: Me

The different ways my roads converged,
The different ways from darkness I emerged,
The different ways I survived when I couldn't see,
That has made all the difference to me.

The roads I've traveled and the times I've failed,
The ways I've run when I felt compelled,
The one time in 20 years I actually stopped to breathe,
That has made all the difference to me.

When I accepted help and took a chance,
When I stepped into an unknown circumstance,
When I found light and started to finally be,
That has made all the difference to me.

And for the new paths that I have and will take,
For the person I am now and will awake,

Forever grateful for the struggles that set me free,

That has made all the difference to me

Yes, that has made all the difference to me.

May 13, 2024:
Letting Go

Purging the darkness in my soul

Letting go of baggage

From long ago

Journals, letters, photos and more

Remnants of a life

My life from before

An old me I don't wish to remember

All darkness, tears, and pain

It was time to surrender

So I shed this layer and let it go

So many black bags filled

With overflow

And I walked away feeling lighter

I walked away

Feeling my spirit get brighter

Took a long time to let it all go

I've got more healing to do

But I'm making more room in my soul

June 17, 2024

Blank paper, paints, and pens

Out of my head running head first into pretend

Letting my imagination start to run free

Letting me let go and to just be

Silencing the demons

Luring them to sleep

While I get lost in artistic pursuits

Getting lost in colors deep

Time melts and I feel a release

As my wild mind finds some peace

July 29, 2024

So many endings
From which new visions have sprung

So many doors closed
From which I've emerged and begun

So many times
I have left breadcrumbs in my wake

So many times
I was lost and made mistakes

But for each end
There was a new beginning

For each end
The world kept on spinning

Never did I get so lost
I couldn't find my way back

So I kept on breathing
And found a way to stay on track

So many endings

So many new beginnings

So many hard choices

But in this game I need to keep on winning

December 16, 2024

Forty trips around the sun
Now I see that I have won
Jagged puzzle pieces have fallen into place
Most days I genuinely wear a smile on my face
The mask has been hung and been put away
The demons ask less to come out and play
A dark abyss that called to me for so long
Has shrunken as I have righted so many wrongs
There is more light now than there is dark
But fears are still fears that can arise at a spark
I face challenges now that shake me to my core
But there is no end-all and nothing is like before
I am surrounded by family, support, and love
And I won't let anyone my decisions judge
I do what is the best and healthiest for me
As I continue to fly and be free

About the Author

Joan Rachel Maydet is originally from Northern New Jersey, spending some of her childhood in Connecticut and the Bronx. She now lives on the East End of Long Island. She is a poet, singer, songwriter, mental health advocate, and artist. Her favorite mediums to work in are watercolor and colored pencil. To view her artwork please visit http://www.joanrachelart.com .

Joan and her husband, Mike have a band called Noctiphany. Most of the songs they have composed are inspired by poems they have written and are about recovery and mental health. One song in particular is called "Healing". You can hear their music on http://noctiphany.bandcamp.com .

www.ingramcontent.com/pod-product-compliance
Lightning Source LLC
LaVergne TN
LVHW022220200926
848481LV00006B/2041
* 9 7 9 8 3 4 8 3 7 1 5 8 6 *